What

I

Learned

From

a

Dog

www.invisibletemple.com

Printed in New England

I've written some pretty serious books.

Two decades later, the world itself has become too serious a place. I feel it is my duty to address the situation by writing, or more accurately, compiling a book that offers solace, levity, reflection, self-empowerment and inner joy in these times of stress. Mark Twain once said, "I can live for two months on one good compliment." And he was right. When the fire within is extinguished and motivation is spent, we grasp outside for a spark to regenerate our self worth. I collected the following inspirations, quotations and invocations over the years,  specifically during a difficult and dark time in my own life. Some are attributed, some I created, and many were written anonymously. Regardless of origin, they helped to raise me off the ground, even prevented me from ending up under it. And therein lies the intent behind this humble tome: May it motivate and sustain you when your eyes open to another dawn and the experience it brings.

There's no set direction. You can read it forwards, backwards, or simply dive in as the mood dictates. The important thing is to take any page and make its message your mantra for the day.

I feel I've reached the top floor of my own building, so the best I can offer is to send the elevator back down to assist those on the way up.

— *Freddy Silva, somewhere between London and Wellington*

RECIPE FOR HAPPINESS.
KHABAROVSK OR ANYPLACE

One grand boulevard with trees
with one grand cafe in sun
with strong black coffee in very small cups.

One not necessarily very beautiful
man or woman who loves you.

One fine day.

— Lawrence Ferlinghetti

An optimist is someone who goes after Moby Dick in a rowboat and takes the tartar sauce with him.

— Zig Ziglar

Death is not the greatest loss in life.
The greatest loss is what dies
within us while we live.

— anon

Help others get ahead. You will always
stand taller with someone else
on your shoulders.

— Bob Moawad

If opportunity doesn't knock, build a door.

— *Milton Berle*

CHANGE

But start slowly,
because the direction is more important
than the speed.

Sit on another chair,
at the other side of the table.
Later on, sit at another table.

When you go out,
walk on the other side of the street.
Later on take another route,
walk on other streets,
calmly,
observing with attention
the places you pass by.

Take another bus.
For a while, change the style of your clothing.
Give up your old shoes.
Walk barefoot for a few days.

Take a whole afternoon
to roam freely in the fields,
or in the park

and listen to the song of birds.
Watch the world from other perspectives.
Open and close the drawers
and doors with your left hand.

Sleep on the other side of bed.
Later on, try to go to sleep in
other beds in the house.

Watch different TV programmes,
buy other newspapers.
Read other books,
Live other romances.

Don't let habit become a life style.
Love what is new.
Go to bed later.
Go to bed earlier.

Learn a new word per day
in another language.
Correct your posture.
Eat a bit less,
choose different food,
different seasonings,
new colours, new delicacies.

Try something new every day,
a new method,

a new flavour,
a new pleasure,
a new love.
A new life.

Try.
Make new friends.
Try new loves.
Build new relationships.

Have lunch in other places,
go to other restaurants,
have another type of drink,
buy bread from another bakery.
Have lunch earlier
have dinner later. Or vice versa.

Choose another grocery store,
another type of soap,
another tooth paste,
take a shower at different times.

Use pens in different colours.
Take walks in different places.
Love a lot,
more and more,
in different ways.

Change your handbag,

your wallet,
your travelling bags,
change your car,
buy new spectacles,
write verses and poems.

Throw away the old watches,
break delicately
those harsh alarm clocks.

Open an account at a different bank.
Go to other cinemas,
other beauty salons,
other theatres,
visit new museums.

Change.
Remember that Life is precious.
Think seriously about getting another job,
a lighter type of work,
with more pleasure,
more dignity,
a more humane work.

If you do not find reasons to be free,
invent them.
Be creative.
Cry out as loud as you can in the open air.

Let others think you are crazy.

Take the chance to go on a long
unpretentious trip,
if possible without destination.

Experience new things.
Change again.
Try the new.
Experiment once again.

You certainly will get to know better
and worst things than the ones you already knew,
but this is not what matters.
What really matters is the change,
the movement,
the dynamism,
the energy.
The positivity that you are feeling now.

Only what is dead does not change!

I repeat, for the pure joy of living.
Salvation takes place with risk taking,
without which
life is not worth while!

— *Clarice Lispector*

Success is not measured by what one brings but rather by what one leaves.

You can't change the wind.
However, you can adjust your sails.

MEMO FROM GOD

Effective immediately, please be aware that there are changes you need to make in your life. These changes need to be completed in order that I may fulfill my promises to you to grant you peace, joy and happiness in this life. I apologize for any inconvenience, but after all that I am doing, this seems very little to ask of you. I know, I know, I already gave you a number of Commandments. Keep them. But follow these guidelines as well.

1. QUIT WORRYING. Life has dealt you a blow and all you do is sit and worry. Have you forgotten that I am here to take all your burdens and carry them for you?

2. PUT IT ON THE LIST. Something needs done or taken care of. Put it on the list. No, not YOUR list. Put it on MY to-do-list. Let ME be the one to take care of the problem for you.

3. TRUST ME. Once you've given your burdens to me, quit trying to take them back. Trust in me. Have the faith that I will take care of all your needs, your problems and your trials. I want to help you. All you have to do is ask.

4. LEAVE IT ALONE. Don't wake up one morning and say, "Well, I'm feeling much stronger now, I think I can handle it from here." Why do you think you are feeling stronger now? It's simple. You gave me your burdens and I'm taking care of them. Leave them with me and forget about them. Just let me do my job.

5. TALK TO ME. I want you to forget a lot of things. Forget what was making you crazy. Forget

the worry and the fretting because you know I'm in control. But there's one thing I pray you never forget. Please don't forget to talk to me — often. I love you. I want to hear your voice.

6. HAVE FAITH. I see a lot of things from up here that you can't see from where you are. Have faith in me that I know what I'm doing.

7. SHARE. You were taught to share when you were only two years old. When did you forget? That rule still applies.

8. BE PATIENT. I managed to fix it so in just one lifetime you could have so many diverse experiences. You grow from a child to an adult, have children, change jobs many times, learn many trades, travel to so many places, met thousands of people, and experience so much. Trust in my timing, for my timing is perfect.

9. BE KIND. Be kind to others, for I love them just as much as I love you.

10. LOVE YOURSELF. As much as I love you, how can you not love yourself? You were created by me for one reason only - to be loved, and to love in return.

I am a God of Love. Love me. Love your neighbors. But also love yourself. It makes my heart ache when I see you so angry with yourself when things go wrong. You are very precious to me. Don't ever forget that.

With all my heart I love you,

G

"When I despair, I remember that all through history the way of truth and love has always won. There have been tyrants and murderers and, for a time, they can seem invincible but, in the end, they always fall. Think of it – always."

— *Mahatma Gandhi*

The most destructive habit: worry

The greatest joy: giving

The greatest loss: self respect

The most satisfying work: helping others

The ugliest personality trait: selfishness

The most endangered species: dedicated leaders

The greatest natural resource: youth

The greatest drink: encouragement

The greatest problem to overcome: fear

The most effective sleeping pill: peace of mind

The most crippling disease: excuses

The most dangerous outcast: a gossip

The best computer: the brain

The worst thing to be without: hope

The deadliest weapon: the tongue

The two most powerful words: I can

The greatest asset: faith

The most worthless object: self pity

The most powerful telephone: prayer

The most beautiful attire: a smile

The most prized possession: integrity

The most contagious spirit: enthusiasm

The most powerful force: love

Here is a test to find whether your mission
on earth is finished: If you are alive, it isn't.

— *Richard Bach*

RIGHT NOW

somebody is thinking of you

somebody is caring about you

somebody misses you

somebody wants to talk to you

somebody wants to be with you

somebody hopes you aren't in trouble

somebody is thankful for the support you provided

somebody wants to hold your hand

somebody hopes everything turns out all right

somebody wants you to be happy

somebody wants you to find him/her

somebody is celebrating your successes

somebody wants to give you a gift

somebody thinks that you are a gift

somebody loves you

somebody admires your strength

somebody is thinking of you and smiling

somebody wants to be your shoulder to cry on

ADVICE

Don't try so hard, the best things come when you
least expect them to.

Make yourself a better person and know who you are
before you try and know someone else and expect
them to know you.

There's always going to be people that hurt you,
so what you have to do is keep trusting and just be
more careful about who you trust next time around.

Maybe God wants us to meet a few wrong people
before meeting the right one, so that when we finally
meet the person, we will know how to be grateful.

Don't waste your time on a man/woman who
isn't willing to waste their time on you.

To the world you may be one person, but to
one person you may be the world.

Never frown, even when you are sad, because you
never know who is falling in love with your smile.

The worst way to miss someone is to be sitting
right beside them knowing you can't have them.

A true friend is someone who reaches for your
hand and touches your heart.

Just because someone doesn't love you the way
you want them to, doesn't mean they don't love you
with all they have.

No man or woman is worth your tears, and the
one who is, won't make you cry.

Don't cry because it is over, smile because
it happened.

— anon

Smart is when you believe
only half of what you hear.

Brilliant is when you know
which half to believe.

— *anon*

Never sacrifice a principle for a temporary gain.

— anon

Success seems to be connected with action.
Successful people keep moving.
They make mistakes but they never quit.

— Conrad Hilton

if

If you have food in the refrigerator,
clothes on your back, a roof overhead and
a place to sleep, you are richer than 75% of
this world.

If you have money in the bank, in your
wallet, and spare change in your pocket,
you are among the top 8% of the wealthy.

If you woke up this morning with more
health than illness, you are more blessed
than the million who will not survive
the week.

If you have never experienced the danger of
battle, the loneliness of imprisonment, the
agony of torture, or the pangs of starvation,
you are ahead of 500 million people.

If you can attend a church meeting
without fear of harassment, arrest, torture,
or death, you are more blessed than
three billion people.

If you hold up your head with a smile on
your face and are truly thankful, you are
blessed because the majority can,
but most do not.

If you can hold someone's hand, hug them
or even touch them on the shoulder, you
are blessed because you can offer
healing touch.

If you can read this, you are more blessed
than two billion people who cannot read
at all.

Count your blessings.

Let us live so that when we come to die even the undertaker will be sorry.

— *Mark Twain*

DUST IF YOU MUST

Dust if you must, but wouldn't it
be better to paint a picture or
write a letter,
bake a cake or plant a seed,
ponder the difference between
want and need?

Dust if you must, but there's not much time,
with rivers to swim and mountains to climb,
music to hear and books to read,
friends to cherish and life to lead.

Dust if you must, but the world's out there
with the sun in your eyes, the wind in your hair,
a flutter of snow, a shower of rain.
This day will not come around again.

Dust if you must, but bear in mind,
old age will come and it's not always kind.

And when you go and go you must —
you, yourself, will make more dust!

— Rose Milligan

People are like stained-glass windows.
They sparkle and shine when the sun is out,
but when the darkness sets in, their true beauty
is revealed only if there is a light from within.

— *Elisabeth Kubler-Ross*

FAILURES

'Tis better to have tried in vain,
  Sincerely striving for a goal,
Than to have lived upon the plain
  An idle and a timid soul.
'Tis better to have fought and spent
  Your courage, missing all applause,
Than to have lived in smug content
  And never ventured for a cause.
For he who tries and fails may be
  The founder of a better day;
Though never his the victory,
  From him shall others learn the way.

— *Edgar A. Guest*

I have had dreams and I have had nightmares.
I overcame the nightmares because of my dreams.

— *Dr. Jonas Salk*

Without leaps of imagination, or dreaming,
we lose the excitement of possibilities.
Dreaming, after all, is a form of planning.

— *Gloria Steinem*

Fall seven times, stand up eight.

— *Japanese Proverb*

A cloudy day is no match for a
sunny disposition.

— *William Arthur Ward*

The most powerful weapon on earth is
the human soul on fire.

— *Marshall Foch*

Three things cannot be long hidden: the sun, the moon, and the truth.

Nothing can harm you as much as your own thoughts unguarded.

Wear your ego like a loose fitting garment.

Do not depend on others for sanctuary or salvation.

If you find no one to support you on the spiritual path, walk alone.

All that we are is the result of what we have thought.

Ambition is like love: impatient both of delays and rivals.

Endurance is one of the most difficult disciplines. But it is to the one who endures that the final victory comes.

One moment can change a day, one day can change a life, and one life can change the world.

True love is born from understanding.

What we are today comes from our thoughts of yesterday, and our present thoughts build our life of tomorrow.

Those who cling to perceptions and views wander the world offending people.

An idea that is developed and put into action is more important than an idea that exists only as an idea.

Better it is to live one day seeing things rise and fall than to live a hundred years without ever seeing things rise and fall.

He who sits alone, sleeps alone, and walks alone, who is strenuous and subdues himself alone, will find delight in the solitude of the forest.

The way is not in the sky. The way is in the heart.

If you do not change direction, you may end up where you are heading.

Everything in moderation, including moderation.

— Gautama Buddha

Remember that overnight success
usually takes about 15 years.

LESSONS

I've learned...
That the best classroom in the world is at the feet
of an elderly person.

I've learned...
That when you're in love, it shows.

I've learned...
That just one person saying
"You've made my day!" makes mine.

I've learned...
That being kind is more important
than being right.

I've learned...
That no matter how serious your life requires you
to be, everyone needs a friend to act goofy with.

I've learned...
That sometimes all a person needs is a hand to
hold and a heart to understand.

I've learned...
That life is like a roll of toilet paper. The closer it
gets to the end, the faster it goes.

I've learned...
That we should be glad we don't get everything
we ask for.

I've learned...
That money doesn't buy class.

I've learned...
That under everyone's hard shell is someone
who wants to be appreciated.

I've learned...
That the Source didn't build Earth in one day.
What makes me think I can?

I've learned...
That to ignore the facts does not change
the facts.

I've learned...
That the easiest way to grow is to surround
yourself with people who are smarter.

I've learned...
That no one is perfect until you
fall in love with them.

I've learned...
That life is tough, but I'm tougher.

I've learned...
That the less time I have to work with,
the more things I get done.

I've learned...
That one should keep their words soft and
tender, because tomorrow you may have to
eat them.

I've learned...
That a smile is an inexpensive way to improve
your looks.

I've learned...
That someone will take the opportunities
you neglect.

I've learned...
That when you harbour bitterness,
happiness will dock elsewhere.

I've learned...
That everyone wants to live on top of the
mountain, but all the growth takes place
at the foot, in the soil.

Change is inevitable.
Growth, however, is optional.

We can learn a lot from crayons. Some are sharp, some are pretty, some are dull, some have weird names, and all are different colors, but they all have to learn to live in the same box.

— *anon*

If you assume a very small, infinitely small level of being, then everything appears to be outside you. That's maximum separation from awareness. You have become a physical particle! On the other hand, if you assume a level of being and openness that is expansive enough to contain the universe, then the universe is within you.

— *Harry Palmer*

Handwritten on the wall of Mother Teresa's room

People are often unreasonable, illogical, and self-centered;
Forgive them anyway.

If you are kind, people may accuse you of ulterior motives;
Be kind anyway.

If you are successful, you will win some false friends,
and some true enemies;
Be successful anyway.

If you are honest and frank, people may cheat you;
Be honest and frank anyway.

What you spend years building, someone could
destroy overnight;
Build anyway.

If you find serenity and happiness, they may be jealous;
Be happy anyway.

The good you do today, people will often forget tomorrow;
Do good anyway.

Give the world the best you have, and it may never be enough;
Give the world the best you have anyway.

You see, in the final analysis, it is between you and God.
It was never between you and them anyway.

Treat your friends as you do your pictures.
Place them their best light.

— *Jennie Jerome Churchill*

A candle that lights another candle loses nothing.

— *anon*

Obstacles are what you see when
you take your eyes off your goals.

— Anthony Robbins

The bravest thing you can do when you are not
brave is to profess courage and act accordingly.

— Corra May Harris

MUD PUDDLES & DANDELIONS

When I look at a patch of dandelions,
I see a bunch of weeds that are going to
take over my yard.
My kids see flowers for Mom and blowing
white fluff you can wish on.

When I look at an old drunk and he smiles at me,
I see a smelly, dirty person who probably wants
money and I look away.
My kids see someone smiling at them and they
smile back.

When I hear music I love,
I know I can't carry a tune and don't have much
rhythm so I sit self-consciously and listen.
My kids feel the beat and move to it. They sing out
the words. If they don't know them, they make up
their own.

When I feel wind on my face,
I brace myself against it. I feel it messing up my
hair and pulling me back when I walk.
My kids close their eyes, spread their arms and fly
with it, until they fall to the ground laughing.

When I pray,
I say thee and thou and grant me this, give me that.
My kids say, "Hi God! Thanks for my toys and my
friends. Please keep the bad dreams away tonight.
Sorry, I don't want to go to Heaven yet. I would
miss my Mommy and Daddy."

When I see a mud puddle,
I step around it. I see muddy shoes and dirty carpets.
My kids sit in it. They see dams to build, rivers to
cross and worms to play with.

I wish you mud puddles and dandelions.

Fools look to tomorrow; wise people use tonight.

— *Scottish proverb*

Don't worry about the world coming to
an end today. It's already tomorrow
in Australia.

— *Charles Schultz*

Manifestation is not magic. It is a process of
working with natural principles and laws
in order to translate energy from one level
of reality to another.

— David Spangler

Efforts and courage are not enough without
purpose and direction.

— John F. Kennedy

OUR DEEPEST FEAR

Our deepest fear is not that we are inadequate.

Our deepest fear is that we are powerful beyond measure.

It is our light, not our darkness, that frightens us.

We ask ourselves, who am I to be brilliant, gorgeous, talented and fabulous?

Actually, who are you not to be?

You are a child of God.

Your playing small doesn't serve the world.

There's nothing enlightened about shrinking so that other people won't feel insecure around you.

We were all born to manifest the glory of God within us.

It's not just some of us; it's in everyone.

And as we let our own light shine, we unconsciously give other people permission to do the same.

As we are liberated from our fear, our presence automatically liberates others.

— *Marianne Williamson*

We don't need more money, we don't need greater success or fame, we don't need the perfect body or even the perfect mate. Right now, at this very moment, we have a mind, which is all the basic equipment we need to achieve complete happiness.

— *Dalai Lama*

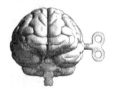

First you fuel the desire,
then the desire will fuel you.

— *Napoleon Hill*

All life is an experiment.
The more experiments
you make, the better.

— *Ralph Waldo Emerson*

PARADOX OF OUR AGE

The paradox of our time in history is that we have taller buildings but shorter tempers, wider freeways, but narrower viewpoints. We spend more, but have less. We buy more, but enjoy less. We have bigger houses and smaller families, more conveniences, but less time.

We have more degrees but less sense, more knowledge, but less judgment, more experts, yet more problems, more medicine, but less wellness. We drink too much, smoke too much, spend too recklessly, laugh too little, drive too fast, get too angry, stay up too late, get up too tired, read too little, watch TV too much, and pray too seldom. We have multiplied our possessions, but reduced our values. We talk too much, love too seldom, and hate too often.

We've learned how to make a living, but not a life. We've added years to life not life to years. We've been all the way to the moon and back, but have trouble crossing the street to meet a new neighbor. We conquered outer space but not inner space. We've done larger things, but not better things.

We've cleaned up the air, but polluted the soul. We've conquered the atom, but not our prejudice.

We write more, but learn less. We plan more, but accomplish less. We've learned to rush, but not to wait. We build more computers to hold more information, to produce more copies than ever, but we communicate less and less.

These are the times of fast foods and slow digestion, big men and small character, steep profits and shallow relationships. These are the days of two incomes but more divorce, fancier houses but broken homes. These are days of quick trips, disposable diapers, throw-away morality, one night stands, overweight bodies, and pills that do everything from cheer to quiet to kill.

It is a time when there is much in the showroom window and nothing in the stockroom. A time when technology can bring this letter to you, and a time when you can choose either to share this insight, or to just hit delete.

— *Bob Morehead*

Go often to the house of a friend,
for weeds choke the unused path.

— *anon*

Never look down on anybody unless
you are going to help them up.

— *Rev. Jesse Jackson*

Although the world is full of suffering,
it is also full of the overcoming of it.

— *Helen Keller*

PEOPLE WHO LOVE YOU

At least two people in this world love you
so much they would die for you.

At least fifteen people in this world
love you in some way.

The only reason anyone would hate you
is because they want to be just like you.

A smile from you can bring happiness
to anyone, even if they don't like you.

Every night, someone thinks about you
before they go to sleep.

If not for you, someone may not be living.

Someone you don't even know loves you.

When you think the world has turned its
back on you, take a look, you most likely
turned your back on the world.

When you think you have no chance of
getting what you want you probably
won't get it, but if you believe in yourself,
sooner or later you will.

Forget about the rude remarks and
remember the compliments you received.

The dogs bark but the caravan moves along.

— *Portuguese proverb*

There is nothing more difficult to plan,
more doubtful of success, nor more dangerous
to manage than the creation of a new system.
For the initiator has the enmity of all who
would profit by the preservation of the old
system and merely lukewarm defenders in
those who would gain by the new one.

— *Machiavelli*

You've got to jump off cliffs all the time and
build your wings on the way down.

— *Ray Bradbury*

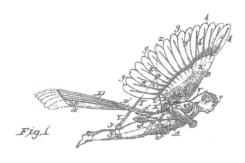

Fig.1

A Test

1. Name the five wealthiest people
   in the world.

2. Name the last five Nobel Prize winners.

3. Name the last five winners of the
   Miss World contest.

4. Name ten people who have won
   the Pulitzer prize.

5. Name the last five Academy Award
   best actor and actress.

6. Name the last decade's worth of
   World Cup winners.

How did you do?

The point is, no one remembers the headliners
of yesterday even though they are the best in
their fields. But the applause dies. Awards
tarnish. Achievements are forgotten. Accolades
and certificates are buried with their owners.

Here's another test

1. List a few teachers who aided
   your journey through school.

2. Name three friends who helped
   you through a difficult time.

3. Name five people who taught
   you something worthwhile.

4. Think of a few people who made
   you feel appreciated and special.

5. Think of five people you enjoy
   spending time with.

6. Name half a dozen heroes whose
   stories inspired you.

The lesson

Easier? The people who make a difference in your life are not the ones with the most credentials, the most money, or the most awards. They are the ones that care.

After we have harnessed the winds,
the waves, the tides and gravity,
we shall harness the energy of love
and then for the second time in the
history of humankind we shall have
discovered Fire.

— *Teilhard De Chardin*

We did not all come over on the same ship
but we are all in the same boat.

— *Bernard Baruch*

I can live for two months on one good
compliment.

— *Mark Twain*

I AM THE DECISIVE ELEMENT

It is my personal approach that creates the climate.
It is my daily mood that makes the weather.
I possess tremendous power to make life
miserable or joyous.
I can be a tool of torture or an instrument
of inspiration.
I can humiliate or humor, hurt or heal.
In all situations, it is my response that decides
whether a crisis will be escalated or de-escalated,
and a person is humanized or de-humanized.
If we treat people as they are, we make them worse.
If we treat people as they ought to be, we help them
become what they are capable of becoming.

— after Haim Ginott

There is no failure except in no longer trying.

— *Elbert Hubbard*

Success is keeping a positive attitude when people fail to keep their promises.

No one ever procrastinated their way to the top.

RULES FOR BEING HUMAN

1. You will receive a body. You may like it or hate it, but it will be yours for the entire period this time around.

2. You will learn lessons. You are enrolled in a full-time informal school called Life. Each day in this school you will have the opportunity to learn lessons.

3. You may like the lessons or you may think them irrelevant & stupid.

4. There are no mistakes, only lessons. Growth is a process of trial and error — experimentation.
The 'failed' experiments are as much a part of the process as the experiment that ultimately works.

5. A lesson is repeated until it is learned. A lesson will be presented to you in various forms until you have learned it. When you have learned it, you can go on to the next lesson.

6. Learning lessons does not end. There is no part of life that does not continue lessons. If you are alive, there are lessons to be learned.

7. 'There' is no better than 'Here'. When your 'There' has become your 'Here' you will simply obtain another 'There' that will again look better than 'Here'.

8. Others are merely mirrors of you. You cannot love or hate something about another person unless it reflects to you something you love or hate about yourself.

9. What you make of your life is up to you. You have all the tools and resources that you need. What you do with them is up to you - the choice is yours.

10. Your answers live inside you. The answers to life's questions live inside you. All you need to do is look, listen and trust.

11. You will forget all of this — and you will remember.

Always begin anew with the day, just as nature does.

— *George Woodberry*

Insistence, Persistence & Consistence.

—*Sidney Szydlow*

Faith is taking the first step even when
you don't see the whole staircase.

— *Martin Luther King, Jr.*

SEVEN WONDERS OF THE WORLD

A group of students was asked to list what they thought were the present Seven Wonders of the World. Though there were some disagreements these received the most votes:

1. Egypt's Pyramids
2. Taj Mahal
3. Grand Canyon
4. Panama Canal
5. Empire State Building
6. St. Peter's Basilica
7. China's Great Wall

While gathering the votes, the teacher noted that one student had not yet finished her paper. So she asked the girl if she was having trouble with her list. The girl replied, "Yes, a little. I couldn't quite make up my mind because there were so many." The teacher said, "Well, tell us what you have and maybe we can help." The girl hesitated, then read:

1. to see
2. to hear
3. to touch
4. to taste
5. to feel
6. to laugh
7. to love

No tree has branches so foolish as to fight among themselves.

Live and work each day as though you are going to be hit by a bus tomorrow, but get the heck out of the way if you see one coming.

— *Connie Jones*

THINGS ARE NOT WHAT THEY SEEM

Two traveling angels stopped to spend the night in the home of a wealthy family. The family was rude and refused to let the angels stay in the mansion's guest room. Instead the angels were given a small space in the cold basement.

As they made their bed on the hard floor, the older angel saw a hole in the wall and repaired it. When the younger angel asked why, the older angel replied, "Things aren't always what they seem."

The next night the pair came to rest at the house of a very poor, but very hospitable farmer and his wife. After sharing what little food they had the couple let the angels sleep in their bed where they could have a good night's rest.

When the sun came up the next morning the angels found the farmer and his wife in tears. Their only cow, whose milk had been their sole income, lay dead in the field. The younger angel was infuriated and asked the older angel how could you have let this happen? The first man had everything, yet you helped him, she accused. The second family had little but was willing to share everything, and you let the cow die.

"Things aren't always what they seem," the older angel replied.

"When we stayed in the basement of the mansion, I noticed there was gold stored in that hole in the wall. Since the owner was so obsessed with greed and unwilling to share his good fortune, I sealed the wall so he wouldn't find it."

"Then last night as we slept in the farmers bed, the angel of death came for his wife. I gave him the cow instead.

"Things aren't always what they seem."

The ultimate measure of a man is not where he stands in moments of comfort and convenience, but where he stands at times of challenge and controversy.

— *Martin Luther King, Jr.*

Be curious, not judgmental.

— *Walt Whitman*

ON PEACE...

When the power of love becomes stronger than
the love of power, we will have peace.

— Jimi Hendrix.

Mental violence has no potency and injures only
the person whose thoughts are violent.
It is otherwise with mental non-violence. It has
potency which the world does not yet know.

— Mohandas Gandhi

An invasion of armies can be resisted, but not
an idea whose time has come.

— Victor Hugo

There is nothing that war has ever achieved
we could not better achieve without it.

— Henry Havelock Ellis

Great tranquility of heart is his who cares
for neither praise nor blame.

—Thomas á Kempis

A merely fallen enemy may rise again,
but the reconciled one is truly vanquished.

— Johan Christoph Schiller

I keep the telephone of my mind open to peace, harmony, health, love and abundance. Then whenever doubt, anxiety or fear try to call me, they keep getting a busy signal and soon they'll forget my number.

— *Edith Armstrong*

Mankind must put an end to war, or war will put an end to mankind... War will exist until that distant day when the conscientious objector enjoys the same reputation and prestige that the warrior does today.

— *John F. Kennedy*

It is not reasonable that those who gamble with men's lives should not stake their own.

— *H. G. Wells*

Can anything be more ridiculous than that a man would have the right to kill me because he lives on the other side of the water, and because his ruler has a quarrel with mine, though I have none with him?

— *Blaise Pascal*

A human being is a part of the whole that we call the universe, a part limited in time and space. He experiences himself, his thoughts and feelings, as something separated from the rest — a kind of optical illusion of his consciousness. This illusion is a prison for us, restricting us to our personal desires and to affection for only the few people nearest us. Our task must be to free ourselves from this prison by widening our circle of compassion to embrace all living beings and all of nature.

— *Albert Einstein*

It is easy enough to be friendly to one's friends. But to befriend the one who regards himself as your enemy is the quintessence of true religion. The other is mere business.

— *Gandhi.*

Why does the Air Force need expensive new bombers? Have the people we've been bombing over the years been complaining?

— *George Wallace*

All we are saying is,
Give Peace a chance.
— *John Lennon*

THE TROUBLE TREE

I hired a plumber to help me restore an old
farmhouse. He had just finished a rough first
day on the job: a flat tire made him lose an hour
of work, his electric drill quit, and his ancient
one ton truck refused to start.

While I drove him home, he sat in stony silence.
Upon arriving, he invited me in to meet his
family. As we walked toward the front door, he
paused briefly at a small tree, touching the tips
of the branches with both hands.

While opening the front door, he underwent
an amazing transformation! His tanned face
was wreathed in smiles, and he hugged his two
small children and gave his wife a kiss.

Afterward he walked me to the car. We passed
the tree and my curiosity got the better of me. I
asked him about what I had seen him do earlier.

" Oh, that's my trouble tree," he replied. "I know I can't help having troubles on the job, but one thing's for sure, those troubles don't belong in the house with my wife and children.

So I just hang them up on the tree every night when I come home and then in the morning I pick them up again.

Funny thing is," he smiled, "when I come out in the morning to pick 'em up, there aren't nearly as many as I remember hanging up the night before!"

Fear knocked at the door.
Faith answered.
No one was there.

— *anon*

To laugh often and much; to win the respect of intelligent people and the affection of children; to earn the appreciation of honest critics and endure the betrayal of false friends; to appreciate beauty, to find the best in others; to leave the world a little better; whether by a healthy child, a garden patch or a redeemed social condition; to know even one life has breathed easier because you have lived. This is the meaning of success.

— *Ralph Waldo Emerson*

Someone's sitting in the shade today because someone planted a tree a long time ago.

— *Les Brown*

THINGS TO PONDER

Maybe the Creator wanted us to meet the wrong people before meeting the right one so that when we finally meet the right person we will know how to be grateful for that gift.

Maybe when the door of happiness closes, another opens, but often times we look so long at the closed door that we don't see the one which has been opened for us.

Maybe the best kind of friend is the kind you can sit on a porch and swing with, never say a word, and then walk away feeling like it was the best conversation you've ever had.

Maybe it is true that we don't know what we have got until we lose it, but it is also true that we don't know what we have been missing until it arrives.

Giving someone all your love is never an assurance that they will love you back. Don't expect love in return; just wait for it to grow in their heart; but if it does not, be content it grew in yours.

It takes only a minute to get a crush on someone, an hour to like someone, and a day to love someone, but it takes a lifetime to forget someone.

Don't go for looks; they can deceive. Don't go for wealth; even that fades away. Go for someone who makes you smile because it takes only a smile to make a dark day seem bright. Find the one that makes your heart smile.

There are moments in life when you miss someone so much that you just want to pick them from your dreams and hug them for real.

Dream what you want to dream; go where you want to go; be what you want to be, because you have only one life and one chance to do all the things you want to do.

May you have enough happiness to make you sweet, enough trials to make you strong, enough sorrow to keep you human, enough hope to make you happy.

Always put yourself in others' shoes. If you feel that it hurts you, it probably hurts the other person, too.

The happiest of people don't necessarily have the best of everything; they just make the most of everything that comes along their way.

Happiness lives for those who cry, those who hurt, those who have searched, and those who have tried, for only they can appreciate the importance of people who have touched their lives.

Love begins with a smile, grows with a kiss and ends with a tear. The brightest future will always be based on a forgotten past, you can't go on well in life until you let go of your past failures and heartaches.

When you were born, you were crying and everyone around you was smiling. Live your life so that when you die, you are the one who is smiling and everyone around you is crying.

PRESENT

Make me an instrument of peace.

Where there is hatred, let me bring love.

Where there is injury, let me forgive.

Where there is doubt , let me have faith.

Where there is despair, let me bring hope.

Where there is darkness, let me shine light.

Where there is sadness, let me bring joy.

Past is history, future is mystery, and this moment is a gift.

That is why it's called the present.

A successful person is one who can lay
a firm foundation with the bricks others
have thrown at them.

— *David Brinkley*

A person with a new idea is a crank until
the idea succeeds.

— *Mark Twain*

You cannot be lonely if you like the
person you're alone with.

— *Wayne Dyer*

WHICH ONE ARE YOU

A young woman went to her mother and told her about her life and how things were so hard for her. She did not know how she was going to make it and wanted to give up. She was tired of fighting and struggling. It seemed as one problem was solved, a new one arose.

Her mother took her to the kitchen. She filled three pots with water. In the first, she placed carrots, in the second, she placed eggs, and the last she placed ground coffee beans. She let them sit and boil without saying a word. In about twenty minutes, she turned off the burners.

She fished the carrots out and placed them in a bowl. She pulled the eggs out and placed them in a bowl. Then she ladled the coffee out and placed it in a bowl. Turning to her daughter, she asked, "Tell me what do you see?"

"Carrots, eggs, and coffee," she replied.

She brought her closer and asked her to feel the carrots. She did and noted that they were soft. She then asked her to take an egg and break it. After pulling off the shell, she observed the hardboiled egg. Finally, she asked her to sip the coffee. The daughter smiled as she tasted its rich aroma. Then she asked, "What's the point, mother?"

Her mother explained that each of these objects had faced the same adversity — boiling water — but each reacted differently. The carrot went in strong, hard, and unrelenting. However, after being subjected to the boiling water, it softened and became weak.

The egg had been fragile. Its thin outer shell had protected its liquid interior, but after sitting through the boiling water, its inside became hardened.

The ground coffee beans were unique, however. After they were in the boiling water, they had changed the water. "Which are you?" she asked her daughter.

When adversity knocks on your door, how do you respond? Are you a carrot, an egg or a coffee bean?

Twenty years from now, you will be more disappointed by the things you did not do than by the things you did do. So, throw off the bowlines. Sail away from the safe harbor. Catch the trade winds in your sails. Explore. Dream. Discover.

— *Mark Twain*

The great use of life is to spend it for something that will outlast it.

—William James

There are always risks when you chase after a dream because growth requires that you leave your comfort zone and enter unknown territory.

— Stedman Graham

MAKE YOUR LIFE HAPPY

Make up your mind to be happy. Learn to find pleasure in simple things.

Make the best of your circumstances. No one has everything, and everyone has something of sorrow intermingled with gladness of life. The trick is to make the laughter outweigh the tears.

Don't take yourself too seriously. Don't think that somehow you should be protected
 from misfortune that befalls other people.

You can't please everybody. Don't let criticism worry you.

Don't let your neighbor set your standards.
Be yourself.

Do the things you enjoy doing but stay out of debt.

Never borrow trouble. Imaginary things are harder to bear than real ones.

Since hate poisons the soul, do not cherish enmity, jealousy, grudges. Avoid those who make you unhappy.

Have many interests. If you can't travel, read about new places.

Don't hold postmortems. Don't spend your time brooding over sorrows or mistakes. Don't be one who never gets over things.

Do what you can for those less fortunate than yourself.

Keep busy at something. A busy person never has time to be unhappy.

Last, but not least: To know lasting happiness, get to know the spirit that guides you. Know yourself.

— *after Robert Louis Stevenson*

Blessed are they who can laugh at
themselves for they shall never
cease to be amused.

Do not argue with an idiot.
He will drag you down to his level
and beat you with experience.

"Rabbit's clever," said Pooh thoughtfully.

"Yes," said Piglet, "Rabbit's clever."

"And he has Brain."

"Yes," said Piglet, "Rabbit has Brain."

There was a long silence.

"I suppose," said Pooh,

"that that's why he

never understands anything."

— A.A. Milne

Laughter is the sun that drives winter
from the human spirit.

— *Victor Hugo*

INSTRUCTIONS FOR LIFE

1. Give people more than they expect and do it cheerfully.

2. Memorize your favorite poem.

3. Don't believe all you hear, spend all you have or sleep all you want.

4. When you say "I love you", mean it.

5. When you say "I'm sorry", look the person in the eye.

6. Be engaged at least six months before you get married.

7. Believe in love at first sight.

8. Never laugh at anyone's dreams. People who don't have dreams don't have much.

9. Love deeply and passionately. You might get hurt but it's the only way to live life completely.

10. In disagreements, fight fairly. No name calling.

11. Don't judge people by their relatives.

12. Talk slowly but think quickly.

13. When someone asks you a question you don't want to answer, smile and ask, "Why do you want to know?"

14. Remember that great love and great achievements involve great risk.

15. Call your mom.

16. Say "bless you" when you hear someone sneeze.

17. When you lose, don't lose the lesson.

18. Remember the three R's: Respect for self; Respect for others; and Responsibility for all your actions.

19. Don't let a little dispute injure a great friendship.

20. When you realize you've made a mistake, take immediate steps to correct it.

21. Smile when picking up the phone. The caller will hear it in your voice.

22. Marry a man/woman you love to talk to. As you get older their conversational skills will be as important as any other.

23. Spend some time alone.

24. Open your arms to change, but don't let go of your values.

25. Remember that silence is sometimes the best answer.

26. Read more books and watch less TV.

27. Live a good, honorable life. Then when you get older and think back, you'll get to enjoy it a second time.

28. Trust in God but lock your car.

29. A loving atmosphere in your home is so important. Do all you can to create a tranquil harmonious home.

30. In disagreements with loved ones, deal with the current situation. Don't bring up the past.

31. Read between the lines.

32. Share your knowledge. It's a way to achieve immortality.

33. Be gentle with the earth.

34. Pray. There's immeasurable power in it.

35. Never interrupt when you are being flattered.

36. Mind your own business.

37. Don't trust a man/woman who doesn't close his/her eyes when you kiss.

38. Once a year, go someplace you've never been before.

39. If you make a lot of money, put it to use helping others while you are living. That is wealth's greatest satisfaction.

40. Remember that not getting what you want is sometimes a stroke of luck.

41. Learn the rules then break some.

42. Remember that the best relationship is one where your love for each other is greater than your need for each other.

43. Judge your success by what you had to give up in order to get it.

44. Remember that your character is your destiny.

45. Approach love and cooking with reckless abandon.

If you think education is expensive, try ignorance.

An important trip in life is meeting people half way.

I believe that imagination is stronger than knowledge
That myth is more potent than history
That dreams are more powerful than facts
That hope always triumphs over experience
That laughter is the only cure for grief
And I believe that love is stronger than death.

— *Robert Fulgham*

A MORNING WISH

What can I wish that this day, this year, may bring
to me?
A few friends who understand me, and yet remain
my friends.
Work to do which has real value without which
the world would feel the poorer.
A return for such work small enough not to tax
unduly anyone who pays.
A mind unafraid to travel, even though the trail be
not blazed.
An understanding heart.
A sight of the eternal hills and unresting sea, and
of something beautiful the hand of man has made.
A sense of humor and the power to laugh.
A little leisure with nothing to do.
A few moments of quiet, silent meditation.
And the patience to wait for the coming of those
things, with the wisdom to know them when they
come.

— W. R. Hunt

We have an infinite number of reasons to be happy
and a serious responsibility not to be serious.

All truth passes through 3 stages.
First, it is ridiculed.

Second, it is violently opposed.

Third, it is accepted as being self-evident.

— *Arthur Schopenhauer*

If you think you're too small to make a difference, you've never spent the night with a mosquito.

— *African proverb*

Letting go

To let go doesn't mean to stop caring, it means
I can't do it for someone else.
To let go is not to cut myself off, it's the
realisation I cannot control the other.
To let go is not to enable but to allow learning
from natural consequences.
To let go is to admit powerlessness, which means
the outcome is not in my hands.
To let go is not to care for, but to care about.
To let go is not to fix, but to be supportive.
To let go is not to be in the middle arranging the
outcome but to allow others to effect their destiny.
To let go is not to be protective, it's to permit
another to face reality.
To let go is not to adjust everything to my desire,
but to take each day as it comes and cherish
myself in it.
To let go is not to regret the past, but to grow and
live from the future.
To let go is to fear less and love more.

Turn your face to the sun and the
shadows fall behind you.

— *Maori Proverb*

A hero is no braver than an ordinary man,
but he is brave five minutes longer.

— *Ralph Waldo Emerson*

ON FRIENDSHIP

True friendship is like sound health: the value
of it is seldom known until it be lost.

— *Charles Caleb Colton*

A real friend is one who walks in when the rest
of the world walks out.

Don't walk in front of me, I may not follow.
Don't walk behind me, I may not lead. Walk
beside me and be my friend.

— *Albert Camus*

Strangers are just friends waiting to happen.

— *Mencius*

If all my friends were to jump off a bridge,
I wouldn't jump with them, I'd be at
the bottom to catch them.

Everyone hears what you say. Friends listen to
what you say. Best friends listen to what you
don't say.

A friend is someone who knows the song in
your heart and can sing it back to you when
you have forgotten the words.

Hold a true friend with both your hands.

— Nigerian Proverb

A HOPI ELDER SPEAKS

"You have been telling the people that this is the eleventh hour, now you must go back and tell the people that this is the hour. And there are things to be considered. Where are you living? What are you doing? What are your relationships? Are you in right relations? Where is your water? Know your garden. It is time to speak your Truth. Create your community. Be good to each other. And do not look outside yourself for the leader."

Then he clasped his hands together, smiled, and said, *"This could be a good time! There is a river flowing now very fast. It is so great and swift, that there are those who will be afraid. They will try to hold on to the shore. They will feel they are being torn apart and will suffer greatly. Know the river has its destination. The elders say we must let go of the shore, push off into the middle of the river, keep*

our eyes open, and our heads above water. And I say,
see who is in there with you and celebrate. At this
time in history we are to take nothing personally.
Least of all ourselves. For the moment that we do,
our spiritual growth and journey comes to a halt.
The time of the lone wolf is over. Gather yourselves.
Banish the word struggle from your attitude and
your vocabulary. All that we do now must be done
in a sacred manner and in celebration. We are the
ones we've been waiting for."

Oraibi, Hopi Nation, Arizona

To avoid criticism,
do nothing,
say nothing,
be nothing.

— *Elbert Hubbard*

Opportunity is missed by most people because
it is dressed in overalls, and looks like work.

— Thomas Edison

We can't all be heroes. Somebody has to
sit on the curb and clap as they go by.

— *Will Rogers*

No one is perfect.
That's why pencils have erasers.

The first step is to penetrate the clouds
of deceit and distortion and learn the
truth about the world, then to organize
and act to change it. That's never been
impossible and never been easy.

— *Noam Chomsky*

In a time of universal deceit, telling the
truth becomes a revolutionary act.

— *George Orwell*

A time comes when silence is betrayal.

— *Dr. Martin Luther King, Jr.*

HAPPINESS

... is the ability to overcome problems. It is discipline of one's own mind. It rises from taking things as they come with patience and equanimity, from choice, from living every moment with grace, from not getting what we do not have but rather appreciating what we have.

It grows in our own flowerbed, not in strangers' gardens. It is an ideal of imagination, and the serendipitous result of looking for something else. It is attained not through self-gratification but through fidelity to a worthy purpose.

The biggest obstacle to happiness is to expect too much of it, and since nobody cares if you're miserable, you might as well be happy.

If you want happiness for an hour, take a nap.
If for a day, go fishing. If for a year, inherit a fortune.
If for a lifetime, help someone else.

— *Chinese Proverb*

Happiness and sadness run parallel to each other. When one takes a rest, the other takes up the slack.

— *Hazelmarie Elliott*

THE INVITATION

It doesn't interest me what you do for a living. I want
to know what you ache for, and if you dare to dream
of meeting your heart's longing. It doesn't interest
me how old you are, I want to know if you will risk
looking like a fool for love, for your dreams, for the
adventure of being alive.

It doesn't interest me what planets are squaring your
moon, I want to know if you have touched the centre
of your own sorrow, if you have been opened by life's
betrayals, or have become shrivelled and closed from
fear of further pain. I want to know if you can sit
with pain, mine and your own, without moving to
hide it, fade it or fix it. I want to know if you can be
with joy, mine or your own, if you can dance with
wildness and let the ecstasy fill you up to the tips of
your fingers and toes without feeling that you have to
be careful, realistic, or remember the limitations of
being human.

It doesn't interest me if the story you are telling is
true, I want to know if you can disappoint another
to be true to yourself, if you can bear the accusation
of betrayal and not betray your soul. I want to know

if you can be faithful and therefore be trustworthy. I want to know if you can see beauty even when it's not pretty every day and if you can source your life from God's presence.

I want to know if you can live with failure, yours and mine, and still stand on the edge of a lake and shout to the silver of the full moon, "Yes!" It doesn't interest me to know where you live or how much money you have. I want to know if you can get up after the night of grief and despair, weary and bruised to the bone, and do what needs to be done for the children.

It doesn't interest me who you are, or how you came to be here. I want to know if you will stand in the centre of the fire with me and not shrink back. It doesn't interest me where or what or with whom you have studied, I want to know what sustains you from the inside when all else falls away. I want to know if you can be alone with yourself, and if you truly like the company you keep in the empty moments.

— *Oriah House*

Pain is inevitable, suffering is optional.

— M. Kathleen Casey

Nothing multiplies so much as kindness.

— *John Ray*

To the world, you may be one person,
but to one person you may be the World.

If you think nobody cares if you're alive,
try missing a couple of car payments.

Beware the leader who bangs the drums of war in order to whip the citizenry into a patriotic fervor, for patriotism is indeed a double-edged sword. It both emboldens the blood, just as it narrows the mind.

And when the drums of war have reached a fever pitch and the blood boils with hate and the mind has closed, the leader will have no need in seizing the rights of the citizenry. Rather, the citizenry, infused with fear and blinded by patriotism, will offer up all of their rights unto the leader and gladly so.

How do I know? For this is what I have done.

— *Julius Caesar*

The man who trades freedom for security
does not deserve nor will he receive either.

— *Benjamin Franklin*

To put the world in order,
we must first put the nation in order.
To put the nation in order,
we must put the family in order.
To put the family in order,
we must cultivate our personal life.
And to cultivate our personal life,
we must first set our hearts right.

— Confucious

Growing is a lifetime job, and we grow most when we're down in the valleys, where the fertilizer is.

— *Barbara Johnson*

Gratitude unlocks the fullness of life. It turns what we have into enough, and more. It turns denial into acceptance, chaos to order, confusion to clarity. It can turn a meal into a feast, a house into a home, a stranger into a friend. Gratitude makes sense of our past, brings peace for today, and creates a vision for tomorrow.

— *Melody Beattie*

Don't be dismayed at good-byes. A farewell
is necessary before you can meet again.
And meeting again, after moments or
lifetimes, is certain for those who are friends.

— *Richard Bach*

You won't ever get started if you wait for all the conditions to be "just right."

LESSONS FROM
THE SUMERIAN FLOOD

Don't miss the boat.

Remember that we are all in the same boat.

Plan ahead. It wasn't raining when the Ark was built.

Stay fit. When you're 600 years old, someone may ask you to do something really big.

Don't listen to critics, just get on with the job at hand.

Build your future on high ground.

For safety's sake, travel in pairs.

Speed isn't always an advantage. The snails were on board with the cheetahs.

When you're stressed, float a while.

Remember, the Ark was built by amateurs, and the Titanic by professionals.

Negativity will sink your ship, remove it instantly.

No matter the storm, there's a rainbow waiting.

Not a shred of evidence exists in favour of the idea that life is serious.

— *Bertrand Russell*

WHAT I LEARNED FROM A DOG

Avoid biting when a simple growl will do.

Never pass up the opportunity to go for a joy ride.

Allow the experience of fresh air and the wind in your face to be pure ecstasy.

When it's in your best interest, always practice obedience.

Let others know when they've invaded your territory.

Run, play and do something silly daily.

Eat with gusto and enthusiasm.

Be loyal.

Never pretend to be something you're not.

If what you want lies buried, dig until you find it.

When someone is having a bad day, be silent, sit close by and nuzzle them.

Thrive on compliments and let people touch you.

Live in the moment, leave the past in the past.

Leave room in your schedule for a good nap.

On hot days, drink lots of water and lie under
a shady tree.

No matter how often you are criticized, run right
back and make friends.

Don't hold a grudge.

When you leave your yard, make it an adventure.

Explore everything at least once.

Delight in the joy of simple things.

Stare at someone long enough and eventually
you'll get what you want.

If it's not wet and sloppy, it's not a real kiss.

CREDITS

Marianne Williamson quote, from A Return To Love: Reflections on the Principles of "A Course in Miracles." ©HarperPerennial, 1992

Rose Mulligan's quote appeared in Lady Magazine, 1998

Bob Moorehead published "The Paradox of Our Time," in his 1995 anthology Words Aptly Spoken, ©Overlake Christian Bookstore

Haim Ginott's original quote from Teacher and Child, ©Macmillan 1972

A.A. Milne's quote from Winnie The Pooh, E.P. Dutton, New York, 1926. Illustration by Ernest Shepard

Instructions For Life were predominantly published in Life's Little Instruction Book, by H. Jackson Brown Jr., ©Rutledge Hill Press, 1991

W.R. Hunt quote, from Guidewords: An Anthology of Inspiration and Humor, ©Shawn-Barton, 1971

Oriah House's quote from her book The Invitation ©1999, HarperONE, San Francisco. All rights reserved. Presented with permission of the author. www.oriah.com

Author photo: Irena Stenner

Also by Freddy Silva

Scotland's Hidden Sacred Past

The Missing Lands
Uncovering Earth's Pre-flood Civilization

First Templar Nation
How the Knights Templar Created
Europe's First Nation-state

The Lost Art of Resurrection
Initiation, Secret Chambers and
the Quest for the Otherworld

The Divine Blueprint
Temples, Power Places and the Global Plan
to Shape the Human Soul

Secrets In The Fields
The Science and Mysticism of Crop Circles

Chartres Cathedral
The Missing or Heretic Guide

www.invisibletemple.com

CPSIA information can be obtained
at www.ICGtesting.com
Printed in the USA
BVHW070933160822
644715BV00006B/238